I0169395

Organic, Real and Raw Poetic Expressions for My Sisters, My Girls, My Ladies

Organic, Real and Raw Poetic Expressions for My Sisters, My Girls, My Ladies

Joyce G. Moore

Organic, Real and Raw
Poetic Expressions
for
MySisters, MyGirls, MyLadies

by
Joyce G. Moore

© Copyright 2016

ISBN-13: 9781931259040

ISBN-10: 1931259046

All rights reserved.
This book may not be reproduced,
in whole or in part, through duplication
or any means, without written
permission from the author.

For information contact:
Joyce G. Moore
Life Management Inc.
Post Office Box 1683
Marietta, GA 30061

E-Mail: moorelife08@gmail.com

Printed in USA

Special Acknowledgements

FIRST AND FOREMOST, I wish to give my special thanks to my loving parents. They laid the groundwork for me to be an independent thinker and observer of all things. They showed me that learning extends beyond the structured classroom. For that reason, I have recognized that experiences have been some of my best teachers. I certainly do not discount my ongoing formal education. Formal education is truly a part of the process and part of the equation for continued success.

I continue to be inspired by my mother, who loved to read and shared her wisdom through her writings. I appreciate the sacrifices that my parents made to raise four well-rounded children. I also appreciate my parents for setting a wonderful example of how a loving relationship within a marriage should be. They exemplified how important love, civil communications, fair compromise, trust, respect, support, forgiveness and freedom to pursue ones interests, are all important to sustaining a marital relationship.

I extend my special love to my three siblings, my sisters-in-law and their wonderful children, who are all a true blessing to our close-knit family. Thanks to all of my loving family members and friends. You all continue to inspire me everyday.

I acknowledge and give endless thanks to my loving and most talented husband. For over 50 years, you have continued to be a guiding light and the love of my life. I extend my deep appreciation to you for all of your encouragement and support. You are a shinning example of true manhood.

My special thanks to all of the readers of *"Organic, Real and Raw Poetic Expressions"*. May you find the thoughts expressed to be nuggets of gold and enlightenment for your soul.

Joyce G. Moore

Preface

To MySisters, MyGirls, MyLadies – how about a little "Teaser Poetry" to offer you some "Food for Thought"? These *"Organic, Real and Raw Poetic Expressions"* are tempered with reality, possibilities, and more or less, fictional situations between the sexes.

The "Food for Thought Menu" may consist of "Nourishing Food", "Junk Food", and "Wisdom Food". You may find value within, by spending your precious time to consider which category that you may wish to choose from. By all means, there is no intention to cause indigestion, nor demean the character of anyone – male nor female. The only intent is to offer a variety of nourishment and entertainment for the unique mind and soul.

Not to fear – these poetic expressions are not intended in any way to suggest that "good men" are not a potential part of our female relationships – IF we should find them to be worthy of our love and affection. Yes, IF.

Remember, thoughts, ideas and interpretations do resonate differently, based on our personal experiences, levels of wisdom, degree of maturity and other innate human factors. Many of you may find *'experience to be your best teacher'*. So, we all stand to broaden our horizons by engaging and interacting with a variety of individuals. However, doing so with caution and a degree of guarded optimism, mixed with some wise skepticism.

Keep in mind; "Utopia and Perfection" are both fantasies. To those who are seeking either or both, may your fantasy come to fulfillment.

May you derive great pleasure and greater insight, as you enjoy the "Food for Thought", "Teaser Poetry" from *"Organic, Real and Raw Poetic Expressions for MySisters, MyGirls, MyLadies"*.

Peace, Love and Blessings

Joyce G. Moore

Table of Contents

Why Settle?

Know what you truly want for your own life.
Know if you really desire being single or a wife.
Know that "Mr. Right", to this day, has not been found.
Know that no potential mate has even come around.

Do you feel that time is really running out?
Do you feel as if you could run around and shout?
Do you feel that your life is void of a trusted friend?
Do you feel as if you have reached your wits end?

You may wish to rethink your plan.
You may find that right now you do not really
need a man.
You may consider designing a life just for you.
You may think of so many other things to do.

Why even settle for less than you deserve or want?
Why even settle when friends and family say "Don't"?
Why even settle for the sake of loosing a bet?
Why even settle and live a life of regret?

If you do not settle:
He may magically appear and past the test.
He may be the one who is really the best.
He may be the one who proves to be worth the wait.
He may be the one who just might be a great mate.

So, Why Settle?

Endless Shades of "Self-Love"

There is a special 'color chart',
revealing **"Endless Shades of Self-Love"**.
You can change the shades of you life
as often as you choose.
Use every shade and color of the rainbow,
but please stay away from "the blues".

Try using the various hues on the chart
to mix up unique shades for you.
Each day mix and match different shades
to reflect your loving mood.
Even use various shades of "Self-Love"
in place of unhealthy food.

Feel free to paint upon your "Life's Canvas",
various shades of platinum, silver and gold.
Use every shade that reflects harmony, goodness,
joy, peace, happiness, love and grace.
As you greet others, **"Endless Shades of Self-Love"**
will shine through and reflect upon your face.

Just the Way I Am

I'm truly God's gift to me.
Looking in the mirror, I really love what I see.
Others may attempt to unfairly judge.
I won't waste my time by holding a grudge.

I know that I'm not perfect in any way.
No intentions of allowing 'lack of" to ruin my day.
I've learned to love myself, the way that I am.
Not trying to change me with fancy clothes or glam.

Dressing appropriately for my shape and size.
Must wear styles of dresses below my thighs.
Oh, I avoid wearing anything that is too tight.
Want to keep my extra bulges out of unnecessary sight.

Yes, diets and exercise – they say are a must.
Must do both – do both – before I bust.
Tried them both but they didn't tend to stick.
Guess that is the reason that I am so thick.

Well, there is a moral to this story.
It may not end in some other's glory.
I'm just living my own truth with some disguise.
I've made mental and physical adjustments for my size.

Fill Your Own Glass to the Brim

Fill your own glass to the brim.
Fill it yourself – don't wait for him.
Life is about what you make it for yourself.
So, go ahead – lift that glass from the shelf.

Open your eyes each day – to possibilities a new.
Know that each day you can design a life especially
for you.
Fill your glass with the nectar of your choice.
Not allowing anyone to silence your voice.

Fill your own glass with happiness, harmony
and kindness.
Always remember to fill your glass with peace
and goodness.
Forget not laughter, patience, self-love and grace.
All of life's goodness will overflow into every space.

Also include things that don't even cost a single dime.
Continue to enjoy your life in your own special time.
Slowly continue to **"Fill Your Own Glass to the Brim"**.
Fill it yourself – Do not wait for him.

Catch 22 - What Do You Do?

When faced with a "Catch 22",
and trying to figure out what to do,
and you do not know who to tell.
Just find a quiet place and sit a spell.

In the silence of that very special space,
you are not competing in anyone's race.
So, take your time, exercise your unique wit.
Within a given time, you will "hear" a solution to it.

Not all "Catch 22's" need to cage us in.
Sometimes we just need to find our own peace within.
Make your decisions based on the real facts.
Focusing on irrelevant things may trigger set-backs.

Now, desires of the heart involve more than just you.
So, consider what needs to be done to get you through.
Is there a desire for a solution from the other side?
Maybe neither wants to call a truce because of
too much pride.

What ever your "Catch 22" might really be –
take time to locate the 'Magic Key'.
There is no one answer to solve it all.
Just stay strong – stand tall and do not fall.

Master Your Own Universe

The universe is your own personal world.
You are free to explore it each and every day.
Yes, explore it mentally – at work and at play.

Your unique imagination creates your private world.
You certainly can see things that others may not see.
Such things that may matter to you and not me.

Venture into imaginary places that are beyond belief.
Walk on your own moon – pluck stars from the sky.
Needless to say – no need to explain why.

Challenge yourself to reach a special place of joy.
"Miracles" can spring forth before your eyes.
No longer hidden away or in a disguise.

Abandon all fears of what others might think.
You write the script – with no need to rehearse.
Just continue to be the **"Master of Your
Own Universe"**.

Fulfilling a Dream

Night dreams fill our minds as we sleep.
Some dreams we would love to keep.
If some dreams are really to come true,
this may be entirely up to you.

No dream can come to be without action.
The true motivation is desire and an attraction.
Next is a plan that must really make sense.
Once the blueprint is drawn – work can commence.

So, as with completing a puzzle – all the pieces must fit.
Must maintain tenacity and never quit.
Fulfilling a dream may become a real chore.
Sometimes we get started and it demands so much more.

Now, daydreams happen in our waking hours.
Over these dreams we may have more powers.
Even these dreams may be a little over the top.
Again, you just got to get started and do not stop.

Employ imagination and faith that you will achieve.
Keep in mind that in fulfilling a dream – you
must believe.
Know that many, many others have fulfilled their dreams.
Once you focus and follow-through – it's not as
hard as it seems.

Remember Not to Tell
Keep the Secret to Yourself

If your guy is really great,
and you want to keep him as your mate,
Remember not to tell.

Great guys may be in short supply.
This is one thing upon which you can rely.
Remember not to tell.

If he has the qualities that you seek for yourself,
write a secret note and hide it on a special shelf.
Remember not to tell.

Your girlfriends may want you to tell all.
Just say, "I'm waiting for his call".
Remember not to tell.

Keep the secret as long as you can.
This is one way to keep your man.

**Remember Not to Tell.
Keep the Secret to Yourself.**

Romantic Lover or Just a Friend?

You spot the guy that you have been dreaming of.
He appears to be someone who you could really love.
Should you make an approach and take a chance?
Could this moment be the start of a romance?

With a pounding heart and a flushed face,
would not want this moment to end in a disgrace.
Looks can be deceiving – for goodness sake.
Would not want this encounter to be a mistake.

Approaching a strange guy is not your style.
So, you decide to wait this moment out for a while.
Just giving an innocent glance now and then.
Hope that his body language will dictate to you when.

Oh my – he is finally looking in your direction.
Can't tell if he is conducting his own casual inspection.
You really do wish that he would make the first move.
The timing must be right – to create a natural groove.

Finally, he moves across the room and comes your way.
He appears to be charming and may know what to say.
Now, you take it from here and say how it will end.
Do you want this guy to be a **"Romantic Lover
or Just a Friend"**?

I Gotta Be Me

You be you and I'll be me.
I know the members of my "Family Tree".
Some may call me "Strange Fruit".
To me, I do some things that I think are uniquely cute.

Made the brave decision to fall from grace.
My decision caused many frowns on many a face.
Maybe one day they will manage to come around.
They may come to appreciate the happiness
that I've found.

Folks practice judging the behavior of others.
My family judges are my father, mother,
sisters and brothers.
Not my intention in any way – within my
family to divide.
Just wish that they could understand my personal side.

We can't please everyone in a strange crowd.
But for my special folk – I want to make them proud.
Nothing illegal or immoral but in other ways I'm free.
In the end – please understand – **"I Gotta Be Me"**.

Is My Butt Too Big?

Does the size of my butt really matter?
Who is so concerned?
My butt is in the rear.
My mind is way up top.
My mind is what runs the whole of me.
Unfortunately, my mind is not what others see.

So much concern over a body part.
Some like it big.
Some like it small.
My butt gets lots of attention by living in the rear.
It is hard to keep it out of public sight.
Can't even hide it in the dark of night.

Got more things to think about.
So, forget that I even inquired.
Got a daily life to live.
Can't focus on a body part.
Whose business is it anyway?
No concern over what others may think or say.

Making of a Fantasy

Come on my 'BFF' – let's head to the mall.
We've got to get ready for "Cinderella's Ball".
We are going to go in search of a potential mate.
Or we may decide to attend without a date.

This is not just another fickle thought of mine,
but a unique plan so creatively divine.
We will shop for a designer inspired gorgeous gown.
We will be the very talk of the whole darn town.

We will search for glass slippers – with diamonds on top.
We will be so elegant – that the compliments
will not stop.
We will look so chic that we can't be turned away.
Let's start on this journey on this given day.

We will have our hair styled to flow like silk in the wind.
We will dance the night away – until the music
comes to an end.
Join me in this fantasy – we have nothing else to do.
If we play our cards right – we can make this
fantasy come true.

Note:
This whole idea may just be nominated for the
"Fickle Thought Award".

Perfection Lives in "Utopia Land"

I heard that some girls have been looking for
their "perfect man".
They need to know that he only lives
in "Utopia Land".
This is where they scooped him up
from a body of soil and sand.

Then they placed him in a specially
designed perfect mold.
Every feature was designed
for maximum elegance and perfection.
The body, the mind, the soul
were all created to make the connection.

There is another thing to keep in mind –
he can not exist on earth.
So, travel to "Utopia Land" may be
a bit difficult as of this given day.
To earn a ticket to travel,
the traveler must also be perfect in every way.

So, those in search of their "perfect man",
have work to do – before the trip takes place.
The preparation may take awhile,
much time and an endless number of years.
Trust that they can manage to pull it off,
or come up with more realistic ideas.

I Want You to Know

To MySisters, MyGirls, MyLadies – I want you to know,
this marriage thing may be a bit overrated.
Some guys want to be serviced from head to toe.

They may give just a little.
They may want you to give a lot.
Some do not even attempt to meet in the middle.

You may lose your freedom, personal space or
some tiny vice.
There are other precious things that you may have
to give up.
So, I remind you to think it over more than twice.

On the other hand – things could go just great.
There are those who won't be over demanding.
They are ready and willing to be a loving mate.

Patience is a well learned feminine trait.
So, by having patience – it could pay off in the end.
Continue to practice patience to avoid an
unnecessary debate.

"Take a Little Selfie Time"

Time to take a "Selfie" with your phone off – if you will.
Find the time and a special place to just sit and be still.

No need to bring anyone else along.
Take time to tune into your own favorite song.

Slip away to your favorite peaceful and quiet place.
Create for yourself a very personal space.

Grab your favorite book from the shelf.
Seek out your secret place – just to be by yourself.

Entertain yourself with a special reflective thought.
Think about some special things that life has taught.

You may wish to seek out a tranquil spot near a nice lake.
Enjoy nature's bounty for your own peace sake.

The clock on the wall does silently chime.
So, it's time to **"Take a Little Selfie Time"**.

Big Girls Do Cry

Big girls really do cry.
There are so very many reasons why.

In relationships – they are committed from the start.
So, they may cry from a broken heart.

Expectations may run as high as the sky.
They are expecting to receive "pie from on high".

They are trying to hold on with an insanely tight grip.
Seeing no hope – they weaken and slip.

They receive too much pressure from family and friends.
It hurts trying to keep up with fads and trends.

Looking in the mirror brings sadness too.
Not knowing where to start or what to do.

With so many issues to personally address –
It feels as if life is a hectic mess.

With no real solutions falling in place –
They allow the tears to roll down their face.

Yes, "Big Girls Do Cry".

Set Yourself Free

If you are sad over a break-up,
can't see the potential of a make-up,
don't even practice being sad.
Think about the words of your 'wise ole dad'.

That guy was not the one for you.
Remember, "To thine own self be true".
Can't make something of what is not.
Soon make him the one that you forgot.

Make yourself happy as soon as you can.
If it is to be – you will soon meet another man.
If you don't – don't pout or fret.
You may consider getting a hobby or a pet.

Keep your mind in that happy place.
Design for yourself a special space.
Peace is what you really need.
When peace is lost – replace it with deliberate speed.

Too many die of "a broken heart".
Remember your lines and act your part.
Prevention is the special "Golden Key".
Denounce the hurt and **"Set Yourself Free"**.

Tit-For-Tat

All over the universe,
lovers are playing "Tit-For-Tat".
If you "do dis", then I'll "do dat".

How about we all refrain
from playing such hurtful games.
Let's be more about shouting out loving names.

If relationships are to last,
partners must practice more loving things.
Never try to break another's heart strings.

No more playing insensitive games
of "Tit-For-Tat".
Only continue to roll out the loving mat.

Dining on Diced Carrots (A Love Story)

SAW YOU FROM afar. Your eyes sparkled, your lips glistened. I could feel you bonding with me. We both walked towards the same space. In time, your eyes tenderly met mine. We both uttered not a word. Both turning away in silence, but then, slowly turning back to meet one another face-to-face. Your smile was warm and tender. Your gestures were smooth and manly. I knew that I did not want to speak, not wanting to break the tenderness of the moment, not wanting this moment to flee.

I knew, I just knew, that you were sent down from Heaven for only me. I so wanted to reach out and passionately embrace you. But I only did so in my mind. My imagination took over. As I reached out to embrace you, I was overwhelmed by your return embrace. My eyes closed. My body melted in your arms. Everyone in the crowded space did not even exist. For this magical moment, we were the only ones on this planet. In the background, the most beautiful music played just for us. We slowly danced on soft white clouds. As the music ended, you spoke such loving words, with amazing strength. You communicated with such a positive demeanor.

I had to come to my real senses and snap back to reality. As I opened my eyes, there you were standing there. I extended my hand and you quickly extended yours. You spoke your name and I spoke mine. Beyond that, no other words were needed to express our feelings. What we shared was more like "Love at first sight". It felt as if we both were inclined to 'throw caution to the wind'. I invited you to my home. You accepted. At that point, we abandoned our plans to continue to our original destinations.

As we headed for my home, hand in hand, we both spoke not a word. I began to think what I could serve, as my pantry was bare. I would not allow my anxiety to build. I could only think that it would be wise to let each moment take care of itself. I could not believe that I was allowing a stranger to visit my home. Trusting my intuition had better pay off.

Upon entering my home, you looked around and gave an approving smile. I invited you into the kitchen. Upon opening the refrigerator, it was void of anything that one would offer a guest. I smiled with embarrassment and you smiled too. With only a bag of carrots and a container of clam dip, we dined. We listened to music, we shared our past, we shared our plans for the future and we laughed. We continued to see one another and shortly realized that we should be together as husband and wife.

Both of us discovered that we love the simple things of life. Who would have ever imagined that two people could enjoy one another, with such spontaneous simple offerings?

We are together today. Our meals and our snacks are generous and well balanced. We will always remember that first day and **"Dining on Diced Carrots and Clam Dip"**. Now, for each anniversary, we recreate that simple menu and reflect on that special moment.

***

The moral of this story:

As the folk use to say, "The best made plans of mice and men can often go astray". By allowing for spontaneity and flexibility, we open up our lives to wonderful possibilities. So, as long as both partners agree, the simple things that we do can bring people together and make the relationship thrive and last for a long time

What Is the Reason?

It happened.

***

Why so?
Who's to know?
Someone didn't try.
That may be the reason why.

It happened to me.
Why should that be?
Why should it not?
It may be something that you forgot.

Where is my "Rainbow's End"?
Is it coming around the bend?
Why is the bend so long?
It allows for things to go wrong.

This is winter and it's very hot.
In keeping with winter it is not.
This temperature is out of season
Well, God knows the reason.

Is there a reason for everything new?
From what do we get our clue?
So different are we all.
Just know the reason may be God's call.

Happy to Still Be Alive

(Secrets from an elderly friend)

Have to get up early to 'mow' the hair on my face.
Then I have to get my sagging breast in place.
My butt is sagging
and my feet are dragging.

This old age is causing me much disgrace.
Can't seem to keep things in their proper place.
I know these are 'pose to be the "Golden Years".
Why am I shedding so many old salty tears?

I wrote a letter to God 'bout a week ago.
Got it back saying "God is already in the know".
Having trouble with my bladder and my vision.
Can't go anywhere, can't watch television.

I wish my letter had power to get a helping hand.
All of this old age stuff is too much for woman or man.
I take my medicine like the doctor say I should.
Wonder from the shape I'm in – is it doing any good?

When I sit down, I become glued to the chair.
When I decide to get up – I can't go anywhere.
Well, in spite of it all – it could be a lot worse.
At least my family has not had to call for the hearse.

"Just Happy to Still Be Alive"

Sign Me Up!

If there is a place to go
where kindness is the norm,
Sign me up!

If there is a place to go
where respect is practiced by all,
Sign me up!

If there is a place to go
where love is practiced and not just preached,
Sign me up!

If there is a place to go
where caring speaks to every heart,
Sign me up!

If there is a place to go
where education is a top priority,
Sign me up!

If there is a place to go
where public morality and ethics are not an option,
Sign me up!

If there is a place to go
where health care is given to all,
Sign me up!

If there is a place to go on this earth,
where racism, wars, hatred, killing, rape,
bullying, jealousy,
stealing, adultery, disrespect, high unemployment and
man's inhumanity to humans does not exist,
Sign Me Up!

Just Breathe and Life Will Follow?

It is no doubt that you know that it's true,
that with each breath – there is life.
But the quality of life that you want for yourself
calls for so much more.

Just breathing – of course
and living life to its fullest
calls for some "Special Effects".

So, make up your mind
about what you want for yourself
and creatively get out and do it.

Never Sell Your Soul

Let the mountain top be your goal,
But never sell your soul.
Around every corner waits "The Man".
He will try to trick you if he can.
Take my word my young friend;
Your honor you must work to defend.
Always keep your wits about you.
And, be ever on the lookout for the shrew.
Don't let peer pressure lead you to destruction.
Seek friends who practice positive construction.
You must always keep a level head.
You don't want to live a life of dread.
There are enough folk living in sin.
Don't you ever stoop to that end.

By Joyce G. Moore

Note: This poem was published in
"Stars in Our Hearts"
Progression
Hard Back Publication 2012 – Page 193
World Poetry Movement as a compilation of
individual poems.

My Shadow and I

My shadow and I make a very good pair.
There is my loyal shadow standing there.

It is certainly grand because we never part;
My shadow has been with me from the very start.

Such true dedication is not easy to find.
Sometimes it stands by me and sometimes it
stands behind.

There are times when it does not even make a mark.
But I still know where it is, even when it hides in the dark.

With my shadow, I am never alone;
It makes me feel secure, just like a precious stone.

So, if you begin to feel lonely, look beside or
inside yourself.
You will find a constant partner, which is you
loyal other self.

By Joyce G. Moore

Note: This poem was published in
"International Who's Who In Poetry"
Hard Back Publication 2012 – Page 250
Consisting of a compilation of individual poems

"When" is Now

When I get more money,
I'll live a decent life.
When I get myself together,
I'll find a husband or a wife.

When I learn a better skill,
I'll land a better job.
When I move away from here,
I'll manage to escape the mob.

When I identify how,
I'll begin to live with more hope.
When I improve my self-esteem,
I will stop using dope.

When I begin to love myself,
I'll understand how to love others.
When I recognize the sacrifices of my parents,
I'll surely come to respect fathers and mothers.

When I find more time in my day,
I'll seriously begin to exercise.
When I learn that others struggle too,
I'll not be so quick to criticize.

***

**Do not wait for "When".
"When is Now" – "Now is When".**

Working on Your Plan

You have plans and you even have dreams.
In your mind the ideas keep flowing in streams.

Many others in your midst appear to be going too slow.
You, on the other hand, are anxious to go and grow.

You are willing to go the extra mile.
Still others, sit back, look at you and smile.

There are only twenty-four hours in everybody's day.
Remember, you have the ability to accomplish
and not stray.

Actively use your brain, your imagination, each and
every hand.
As some are living in leisure, you must be **"Working on
Your Plan"**.

Me - Take It All In Stride?

Relationship after relationship – I've reached out to
do my best.
I know darn well that I've been put through the test.

How long must a "Sister" have to turn the other cheek?
Answers, solutions, better advice I now seek.

Heard enough about how I must set my feelings aside.
Darn tired of hearing how I must take it all in stride.

Can't take any more of any man's sadistic abuse.
Ain't going to stick around waiting for a truce.

My feet ain't bound, my hands ain't tied, my brain
ain't dead.
I know it's time for me to move on ahead.

I'm not the first to find myself in this unhappy state.
Others have clung to a pattern of staying with the
wrong mate.

I see the light that will lead me out of this
undeserving space.
I feel a hand reaching out to pull me from this place.

I'm ready, willing and able to make myself a new start.
I'm so determined not to set myself up for another
broken heart.

No longer will I **"Take It All In Stride"**.
I'm moving on along and regaining my pride.

Life is: A Journey Through Time

Here I am – alive and well.
I entered this life through the birth canal.
But still yet – not really knowing who I am.
The care from others must determine my earthly fate.

At the time that I was born – I was turned upside down
and hit on my behind.
I knew the clock was ticking and life's school
of hard knocks was already in session.

I've jumped ahead in time and years.
I have encountered so many trial and tribulations.
"The school of hard knocks" continues to be my
"Alma Mater".

I shall continue on this "Journey Through Time".
Won't even attempt to make anything rhyme.
Life is just a little hard for me.
I ask for your prayers to see me through.
That is all that anyone else can do.

Oh Cruel World

Flanked in misery,
I suffer everyday.
Got to get my mind straight,
so I don't suffer this way.

Running, hiding, constant denial;
Forced to hide my head in sand.
Battling life's causes;
Got to come up with a plan.

Oh Lord….Please have mercy.
Feels like I'm quickly sinking.
Must soon find my exit ticket.
Now, now mind – get to thinking.

Oops, gravity has failed me.
I am now beginning to sadly float.
What a miserable high this is.
I'm on a bumpy cruise – without a boat.

Back in the day when I was a child,
I enjoyed child's play and jumping rope.
Now I'm older but ain't no wiser,
'cause I'm unwisely slipping to using dope.

Can't begin to imagine where to stand
to step out of these "Hard Luck Shoes".
Yea, others keep saying I can change
my own life's status if I chose.

No more cruel life's test on this earth for me.
Oh kind Master – do deliver me from such fate.
Away from the maddening crowd I must go,
to my own far corner – for peace and solitude as my mate.

Too Tired

Too tired of reading all the words;
None resonate with me.
Seeking answers from the pages;
None did the pages ever share.
Too tired of reading between the lines;
Not one lesson learned.

Too tired of focusing my every thought,
to seek enlightenment for my cause.
Seeking answers was my goal,
to receive much needed joy.
Too tired of trying to internalize the thoughts,
on how to live a joyous life.

Too tired to truly understand,
how to unlock the joy within.
Seeking much more out of life;
Want more than the daily grin.
Too tired of all that I have heard.
Just too tired, too tired, too tired.

Plant a Garden in Your Head

Plant a garden in your head
where all good thoughts can grow.
Nurture all those thoughts
to broaden the scope of all that you know.

Plant only those productive seeds
that bring enlightenment as they unfold.
Soon ideas will truly blossom,
bringing joy and harmony to your soul.

Continue to cultivate the fertile soil
with a gentle stroke and precautionary speed.
No need to use harmful chemicals;
For organic mulch is all that you need.

Eliminate the pest and weeds,
with natural things – no matter what you do.
In return for your constant labor,
the fruit will be abundant – to nourish you.

Throughout your day – tend your garden,
then again – just before you go to bed.
Wisely use every intellectual space,
to **"Plant a Garden in Your Head"**.

Whisper in His Ear

Whisper in his ear,

No other heart is so loving.

No other heart is so true.

No other heart can love you,

as much as I do.

***

Now, sit back and watch the **"Whisper"** work.

***

If it doesn't work in his ear,
find another ear to **"Whisper"** into.

Get to Know Me

You only say that you hate me,
because you don't know me.
The thin line between love and hate
must be erased before it is too late.

Some paths cross in some strange ways.
We may come to appreciate those peculiar days.
Those are the days that we tend to ask "Why"?
The answers may come – by and by.

Some are not willing to meet a stranger – they say.
They do have the freedom to do things their way.
However, one never knows who will bring the needed lift.
The one who they may tend to hate may offer a
special gift.

No book should be judged only by its cover.
When we read the wisdom within – there is
much to discover.
"Get to Know Me" as we sip a glass of lemonade.
This is precious time when friendships can be made.

A Place for His Weary Head

Some guys just want a bosom for their weary head.
Some will lie down in just anybody's bed.

Some will try to make their way in by being very cheap.
Others know that the price can be very, very steep.

Their intentions may be real difficult to read.
Just remember – you may not be able to supply
every need.

Some are looking for a place just to win a manly bet.
Some are offering no commitment in exchange for
needs met.

A heavy head may be too much to accommodate.
So, weigh the facts – before it is too late.

Write You Own Script

Go ahead – write your own personal script.
Act in your own staring role.
It is your own personal story – needing to be told.

Tell it all as only you personally can.
Allow yourself to stand out from the rest of the cast.
Feature unique experiences and situations from your past.

Magnify the periods where the greatest lessons
were learned.
Remember that life is the greatest teacher for
each and everyone.
So, write about all of the fabulous things you've done.

Know that you can tell all – just like it really is.
Your mind will open up to see things – as if your
mind has eyes.
Your past will come to life – even to your own surprise.

Cathartic and honest writing can be a way to
heal a broken past.
Allow your thoughts to freely flow – like the free
flowing river.
Share the details that may even cause you
to shiver.

Some aspects of your story may make you laugh
or even cry.
It's your story to be told in your own unique way.
Just get started and **"Write Your Own Script"** today.

Set Your Own Personal Bar

Okay, set your own personal bar.
Set it for yourself.
You may not want to jump too high or too far.

Jumping up may be a tad-bit easy.
Coming down may cause injury or pain.
A hard landing from too far may make you queasy.

The bar that you set can be repositioned by you.
So, being over-zealous may not be too wise.
Keep in mind – "To your own self be true".

Adjudicate your own personal event.
No outside judges will you need.
Design your very own prize – with little money spent.

Know that you will only be competing with yourself.
No one has to be privy to your personal plan.
In the end – you can place your prize on your secret shelf.

So, set your bar high or comfortably low.
Compete at your own personal pace.
Finish at your own speed – be it fast or slow.

"Set Your Own Personal Bar"

A Lady's Prayer

Now I lay me down to rest.
I pray that I will awaken to be my very best.
Heal my imperfections from head to toe.
Let me awaken – energized and ready to go, go, go.

Keep my breast firm and don't let them sag.
I pray that I will not become an old hag.
Erase every age-line and wrinkle in my face.
Don't play a trick and place them in another place.

I pray Dear Lord; Let it not be a "Bad Hair Day".
Send no problems that will increase the gray.
Oh, by the way, lessen my weight by a pound or two.
Exercise? No time – something else to do.

Melt the cellulite from my thighs and my hips.
Let only kind words flow from my lips.
Work magic on the dust, the dirty clothes piled high.
Make all of my problems escape to the sky.

Make my checkbook balance itself – with some
funds to spare.
Hide the credit card balances – so they won't be there.
Let those new shoes that I bought – not press my
painful bunion.
Protect me from pain that makes me cry – like
when peeling an onion.

May I find true love and give love to others – in a
special way.
Protect me from users, cheaters and liars – each and
every day.
Lord, please let me win the lottery – this request is
not about greed.
I really do plan to share it with others who are
in dire need.

I know that this prayer is rather long – with
many requests.
So, I'll be happy if you'll pick to honor the very best.
Things like – keep my family, friends and me, in
the best of health.
From that point – we can all work hard to earn
our wealth.
AMEN

Oops

Squeezed too much toothpaste
out of the tube.
Couldn't force it back inside,
no matter how I tried.
Oops

Made some improper comments,
much to my regrets.
Things said affected folk's pride,
that I should have kept inside.
Oops

Overcooked the meat,
that I placed on the grill.
My intention was to serve my guest,
by nourishing them with the very best.
Oops

I placed my foot on the accelerator,
accelerating at the very wrong time.
The cop was hiding in the thicket.
This speedy move earned me a ticket.
Oops

Didn't pay my light bill for several months.
I blamed the postman for not delivering the bills.
It was truly my negligence and oversight,
that caused me to live for days without light.
Oops

So many things that we tend to do,
that we wish that we could undo.
When the "cat is out of the bag" – not to return,
we can only ask ourselves – what lesson did we learn?
Oops, Oops, Oops

The Handy Girl's Tool Box

The information to follow will serve you just dandy.
Remember, to always keep your "Tool Box" handy.
Don't let any man limit you to just pushing a stroller.
You can have the joy of using a paint brush and a roller.

I'll tell you what you must learn to do.
Always keep your screw-driver ready – to tighten a screw.
For drilling holes – you will need a drill and proper bits.
When drilling the hole – be sure the screw fits.

In your "Tool Box" is a firm hammer – to drive a nail.
You won't have to depend on an unavailable male.
A good pair of pliers – will serve you just well.
You can manage to get many jobs done and sit a spell.

Having an array of tools handy will liberate you.
You will see what needs fixing and know what to do.
Just know that you can be smart, strong, and handy too.
Don't let your gender limit the many things that
you can do.

Naked is Me

Layers after layers have been stripped from my soul.
Each day I work tirelessly to reach my intended goal.

Working from morning 'til night to earn my
earthly keep.
Keep climbing torturous mountains that are
rugged and steep.

I fall nightly on bended knees and pray for strength
and resolve.
Even my strongest faith will not cause every problem
to dissolve.

Too many folk constantly expect the very most of me.
Can't shake any leaves or fruit from a naked tree.

I have bared myself – right down to my very core.
I have nothing else to give. Please don't ask for any more

Can't everyone see?
"Naked is Me".

The Rebel

He is a Rebel who you think that you can tame.
No matter what you say or do – he will always stay
the same.

The Rebel travels life doing only as he sees fit.
Certain habits – he is not ever willing to quit.

He is going to live as a Rebel for all of his years.
Do you want to live your life shedding buckets of
sad tears?

A boat load of "Special Magic" is needed to tame his kind.
He will never allow another to control his "Rebel Mind".

Better you move on to a much tamer mate.
You may stand a better chance of controlling your
own fate.

Been There - Done That

To MySisters, MyGirls, MyLadies,
I'll tell you my stand,
you don't need just any man to hold your hand.

Now, my suggestion to you;
Since God gave you two,
put one hand in the other and walk on through.

Walk through good times,
walk through bad times and times in-between.
Telling you like it is and this is what I mean.

When you find the right one,
who will be there for you,
your intuition will tell you what to do.

I once was young and immature,
I thought that any man would offer a helping hand.
But no other hand will always come through on demand.

"Been There – Done That".
So, now listen to me.
Rely only on yourself and set yourself free.

This Mind of Mine

It's mine – this mind of mine.
It teaches me many things divine.
It teaches me to be kind to self and others too.
Must keep this in mind in all things that I do.

It teaches me to be flexible and free.
It has wise eyes and is able to see.
It sees things up close and things so far away.
It sees in the dark of night and in the light of day.

It teaches me when to stay incredibly still.
It tells me when to say "No" at my own will.
It knows when I must look within.
It knows that is where inner peace will begin.

It was given to me at the very start.
It has to stay active – so that we will never part.
It is mine – **"This Mind of Mine"**.
It's my constant companion and is mighty, mighty fine.

"To Your Own-Self Be True"

I'm telling you the truth.
This is no lie.
Sometimes things really make us cry.

Owning up to the truth may not always offer
instant relief.
Sometimes owning up to the truth may elicit fears.
The repercussions may even cause some to shed tears.

In spite of it all – it is not very wise to hide out behind
a wall of lies.
This can prove to be the worst thing to do.
It has been said, **"To Your Own-Self Be True"**.

No claims are made – that owning up to the truth
will be trouble-free.
There are times when you must allow the truth
to be known.
Know when it's time to express yourself to other
and try moving on.

Mama Called Me a "Hussy"

Mama called me a "Hussy"
when I stopped playing with toys,
when I started liking boys,
when I started wearing lipstick on my lips,
when I started wearing clothes to reveal my hips,
when I started riding with boys in cars,
when I started hanging out in bars,
when I snuck out at night,
when I was not in her sight,
when I wore short dresses,
when I didn't clean up my messes,
when I started switching my butt,
when I started "The Hussy Strut",
when I rolled my big brown eyes,
when I wore shorts that showed my thighs.

***

Fast forward:
I now have a daughter and I see her as a
reflection of a younger me. All and all, I think that I
turned out alright. I will keep an eye on her and continue
to pray that she will turn out alright too.

Super Size Your Joy

We must practice experiencing joy
and manage to do so without the guilt.
We hear of so much sadness,
unrest and turmoil existing all around the world.
We must balance sympathy, empathy and joy
into our daily lives.

It may be a bit difficult to achieve this
as often as we should.
It may help if we can focus more on what is good.
We owe it to ourselves and our universe
to actively emit positive thoughts and actions.
This may very well help to minimize negative attractions.

Think of unique ways to combat sad feelings
and
"Super Size Your Joy"

My Love-Hate Affair

I hate my thick thunder thighs.
I love my big bright brown eyes.

I hate my belly hanging low.
I love my wise mind that is in the know.

I hate my big bad hurting feet.
I love my hair – nice and neat.

I hate my behind sticking out.
I love my face when I don't have to pout.

I hate my clothes that lack a jazzy style.
I love the things that make me smile.

I hate when people act so very mean.
I love my mind that is so keen.

I hate the bad news that reflects society's ills.
I love things that bring good thrills.

I hate when things tend to go wrong.
I love when I hear an uplifting song.

***

Hate is about extreme dislike and disgust.
We serve ourselves well when we take charge and adjust.

Love is about a devotion to something or someone good.
This is the place that we must focus as often as we could.

How Long Will It Take?

How long have you been standing still?
Once a child but now you are grown.
You are standing still – no movement shown.

A wasted life – so sad to see.
Too precious was it given to you – for you to cast it away.
You have no meaningful agenda – just play, play, play.

Neither judge nor jury am I on this earth.
But maybe it is time to get started to assure yourself
a better fate.
You may just want to start something before it's too late.

Do you have a better vision for your future?
If so, **how long will it take** you to come up with a draft?
You may just want to start to develop a meaningful craft.

How Long Will It Take?

My Soap Opera Story

$\mathcal{L}$OOKING INTO THE lives of others is a true fascination and pre-occupation for many. Over the years the "Soaps" grew to accommodate the viewer's thirst for insights into unending drama and human situations.

The "Soaps" have allowed the viewers to experience many personal emotions and to be entertained at the same time. Many fans have even come to accept certain "Soap" characters as a part of their "extended family".

Knowing every detail of the sorted and mixed-up lives of the characters may help some viewers to sort through their own personal lives. Well, what ever it takes, to put our lives in perspective, then, go for it.

Many of the "Soaps" are only history. However, do you belong to the generation of avid fans who remember any of the various "Soaps" that entertained many for years?

***

We have **"One Life to Live"**, and we would like to live it on **"Sunset Beach"**, away from **"The Young and the Restless"**, so that we can enjoy the remaining **"Days of Our Lives"**, with **"The Bold and the Beautiful"**, who want to be directed by **"The Guiding Light"** to **"Another World"** and enjoy some wonderful times **"As the World Turns"** away from **"Port Charles"**, **"General Hospital"** and the problems of **"All My Children"**.

© 1998 and 2016 by Joyce G. Moore

My Own Special Personal Man

He's hidden away in a very special secret place.
He comes out of hiding when I do so command.
He may be a bit short and a tad bit small.
He may not be extremely handsome or tall.

He gives me satisfaction – that is special to me.
He demands nothing at all in return for what he provides.
He keeps every secret that I share with him.
He provides me with relief – such a priceless gem.

He certainly will not present me with any health risk.
He is always within reach – morning, noon or night.
He is patient, gentle, understanding and kind.
One thing that I know for sure – he is personally mine.

Kudos to:
"My Own Special Personal Man"

Wink ~~~ Wink

Redefine the Love Connection

As relationships grow in time,
it may stretch some to the brink.
Thus causing some couples to soon grow apart,
as the love manages to tragically shrink.

The "Love Connection" begins to fray,
as the heart strings have been stressed.
The sparks that first ignited the flames of love,
may soon begin to be put to the test.

The old "Love Connections" must now be set free.
Must make room for what's current and new.
As time marches on – situations also change.
It becomes necessary – to make adjustments too.

It is important to rekindle the flames of love,
in your youth or even in your prime.
So, **"Redefine the Love Connection"** when needed,
to keep pace with changing of conditions and time.

Search Your Soul

Search your soul
for any stress that lives within.
Actively flush out any,
then start all over again.

Embrace more love of all kind,
to truly enhance your life.
Seek out more meaningful ways,
to eliminate internal destructive strife.

Sit quietly and peacefully alone,
in your own special space.
Survey your personal unique mind.
Enjoy this visit to this magical imaginary place.

This is truly a place that is free of all cares.
This is no time for any type of needless hurry.
Inhale feelings of love, harmony and peace.
Exhale any feelings of unnecessary worry.

Now, allow the love, harmony and peace to remain.
Use all that magically nurture your magnificent soul.
Continue to lock in these essential feelings,
by making this your daily goal.

My Fantasy Love Connection

In my head lives a special lover,
possessing my desired perfect human qualities.
Super human, some may venture to say.
"My Fantasy Love Connection" is compiled my way.

Out in the universe is a mother's perfect-loving son.
He is so kind, respectful, trustworthy, God fearing,
employed, financially responsible, fun loving, clean,
humorous, educated, patient and not at all mean.

Not thinking that it is too much to expect of this man.
I can certainly match the qualities that I seek.
So, no intentions to 'just settle' for less than the best.
A timely courtship will reveal if he will pass the test.

Reality whispers, "No perfect man exists on this earth".
Should I tame my expectations and face reality?
No plans to rush to the altar – just to change my
last name.
If this should happen – it would certainly be a shame.

So, in my best judgment – I am willing to wait.
Will continue to enjoy my life, my family and all
that I have.
Not able to predict the future or my given life's fate.
Maybe **"My Fantasy Love Connection"** will not
arrive too late.

When and Will He?

When things begin to change,
will he continue to love you just the same?
When your hair is a mess,
will he cuddle you any less?

When your figure changes course,
will he embrace the changes that he sees?
When your perky breast begin to sag,
will he begin to complain or nag?

When you need him to lend a helping hand,
will he join in and do his part?
When the house work needs to be done,
will he turn around and run?

When the children come on the scene,
will he accelerate his own demands?
When your chores pile up and are out of control,
will he stand up to his husbandly role?

When you feel tired – down and out,
will he just sit around and pout?
When all is said and done,
will he help you to balance work and fun?

"No" and "Stop"

Things may start out with
a mutual hug and/or a kiss.
Beyond this – we must both mutually agree,
or things <u>may not</u> end up in mutual bliss.

I want you men to know,
when I say "NO" – I mean "NO".
This two letter word is understood by a child.
No need for me to explain by acting crazy or wild.

Open those ears of yours and hear.
There is no need for me to say it more than once.
When I say "STOP" – I mean "STOP".
No need to scream or raise my voice to the very top.

Keep in mind that it is my very own
personal right and personal choice.
Again, I strongly remind you,
there should be no need for me to scream or
raise my voice.

**I mean it – when I say,
"NO" and "STOP".**

I Must Make the Most of Me

Although I might admire others,
for their grand qualities that I see.
I'll never be anyone else,
so, I must make the most of me.

Must make no foolish mistakes,
by spending time on wasted thought.
My wisdom I must put into practice,
by being my best – as I've been taught.

Can't waste my precious time,
on unproductive envy, jealousy or hate.
My energy will be spent,
charting a course to improve my fate.

Knowing my current desires for my success,
I shall diligently work – to set myself free.
This is my own precious life,
where **"I Must Make the Most of Me"**.

Master of Disguise

He may be a "Master of Disguise",
forever thinking of ways to get between your thighs.

If you think that you don't want him there,
don't let him touch you anywhere.

If he is not your personal kind of "Dude",
don't even allow any space – for him to intrude.

He may offer flowers, candy or a meal or two,
as ways to affectionately get next to you.

Buy your own pleasures – if you will.
Then enjoy your own personal thrill.

Saying, "No thank you but I can't commit",
may be one way to make him quit.

If this guy just won't stop – you may want to tell a friend,
just in case it comes to an unhappy end.

Get to know the make-up of a **"Master of Disguise"**.
Remember, they can appear in any color, shape or size.

No Fool Am I - Don't Play Me

I'm no fool.
I went to school.
But life has taught me more.

I know how I want to thrive.
This is truly no jive.
Life has taught me how.

I can read and I can write.
Both make me feel alright.
I also talk and text – to get my point across.

I can work and I can play.
I also like doing things my way.
Feel much better when I can – this I must admit.

Time is quickly fleeting.
Don't ever like repeating.
Only have time to say it once.

Would rather not receive or give a reprimand.
I trust that others – will truly understand.
No Fool Am I – Don't Play Me.

The "Ugly Cake" - The Great Contender

The long table was covered with homemade cakes.
All being most beautiful – except one.
The crowd assembled to view each baked delight.
The unique shapes – the vivid colors – were a lovely sight.

But – once cut into – their shapes no longer mattered.
The judges slowly sampled them – one by one.
Now, no longer judged for the beauty that they displayed;
Only flavor, texture, taste and ingredients of which
they were made.

For the fancy decorations and shapes – there
was no reward.
Appealing to the judges' taste was the final obsession.
It mattered not how they first appeared to human eyes.
So, in the end – the **"Ugly Cake"** had the taste that
won the prize.

The moral of the story:
It is not always about visual appearance. How one may appeal to another's taste, often times becomes the obsession.

"Beauty is truly in the eyes of the beholder". A person may turn a blind eye on external beauty and focus more on substance. This is truly the essence and essential part of what determines the true depth of an individual. Or, in this case – the cake.

Shame on Me!

If my life is not working out for me,
Shame on Me!

If my future is being left to sheer chance,
Shame on Me!

If my mind is not being put to its best use,
Shame on Me!

If my happiness is dependent on another,
Shame on Me!

If my sense of humor is allowed to fade,
Shame on Me!

If my personal universe has lost its luster,
Shame on Me!

If my frowns have taken over from my smiles,
Shame on me!

If my joy, happiness, peace and love have vanished,
Shame on Me!

If my purpose for living has turned to dust,
Shame on Me!

If anything in my life is out of balance,
Shame on Me! Shame on Me!

The "Bitch" In and Out of the Closet

"The Bitch in the Closet",
came out to play.
She wanted to really play,
in a most seductive way.

In the bed was her man,
who was sleeping unaware.
He did not even know
that she was standing there.

Standing totally unclad,
with skin as smooth as silk.
She wanted to awaken him,
but not to offer a glass of milk.

Playing out in her head,
was an offer too hard for him to refuse.
If she could not carry out her plan,
there would be no one to even accuse.

She didn't want to blame herself,
because her intent was to spring a surprise.
Her man was not to blame,
because sleep caused him to close his eyes.

The moral of this story is,
you should enlighten your man.
When it does take two,
both must be totally aware of the plan.

Note:
Okay, you may be thinking that she should have awakened
him and carried out her plan. Well, she did it her way. Now,
how do you want to execute your plan?

Seasons

Oh MySisters, MyGirls, MyLadies –
I got to tell you this;
We go through seasons of our lives.

***

One of these days you may find out,
as a baby, you started out wearing a diaper,
then the time may come when you will
be introduced to "Incontinence Pads".
Later in life you will become a fan of inevitable fads.

***

Some folk don't like to share the facts.
Just be forewarned that life does
present us with certain set-backs.

***

We go from wearing tiny bibs,
to needing to wear big bibs.
We go from learning to talk,
to forgetting what we are talking about.

***

We go from drooling,
to not being able to drool at all.
We go from taking tiny baby steps,
to taking bigger baby steps.

***

In the end – when we are even able 'to go',
we celebrate and cheer.
Especially if we manage
to make it through another year.

The Men in My Life

Nick is a real hunk.
He has such a fabulous manly trunk.

Tom is so attractive and handsome.
He would bring a fabulous ransom.

Jim is built truly solid and strong.
Can't find anything that is wrong.

Bob has hands with strong grips.
He knows how to embrace my hips.

Frank has a body that is so ripped.
The first time seeing him – I nearly tripped.

Mark is tall, lanky and slim.
He's in to me and I'm in to him.

All the men in my life
make me feel real good inside.
I'll keep seeing them all,
until forced to decide.

You Bring Out My Emotions

There are times in my life that you bring out my feelings.
There are times when I don't possess the stamina
for such dealings.

You exhibit such a tolerance when I wear my sad face.
You amaze me with your awareness – that I only
need a tender embrace.

I can't make the sadness go away each time you
tell me goodbye.
Thinking of being away from you – causes me to cry.

Parting for long periods of time – I experience
anxieties and fears.
This is why I can't hold back the salty – sad tears.

I understand – that into each life – must come a
little sadness.
It should not be necessary for me to experience
such madness.

When we are apart – I reflect on our parting
engaging kiss.
In deep reflections – it is still you that I truly miss.

I place such deep value and appreciation for
your compassion.
With so much indifference in this world – is this too
"old fashion"?

No matter what it is – let's keep this feeling for you
and me.
I do not wish to live without what I have come to see.

You are truly a rare gem – a uniquely rare find.
Someone of your compassion is truthfully my kind.

The feelings that I nurture are of great joy.
I shall not toss your feelings around like a child's toy.

You have brought into my heart a divine rapture.
Because of this emotion – my love you can truly capture.

We can sit together for hours – in golden silence and
a loving embrace.
So comfortable in your presence – just staring into space.

Our thought are so mutually one – that we don't have
to even speak.
We share a blending of inner voices – that is
exclusively unique.

I think of what we share – as refreshing as April showers.
To deepen the relationship – you even bring flowers.

In making me feel special – you've certainly done
your part.
Because of all that you have done – you've really
won my heart.

You Truly Bring Out My Emotions

Accountability

This is a story about People named:
Everybody
Somebody
Anybody
Everyone
and
Nobody

There was an important job to be done and
Everybody was sure that Somebody
would do it.

Anybody could have done it,
but Nobody did it.

Somebody got angry about it,
because it really was Everybody's job.

Everyone thought Anybody could do it,
but Nobody realized that Everybody
would not do it.

It ended up that Everybody and Everyone blamed
Somebody when Nobody
did what Anybody could have done.

(Original Author Unknown)

The moral of this scenario, is that too often we sit back and expect somebody, anybody, everybody or everyone else to attend to things that we see that need to be done. In the end, nobody does a thing and nothing gets done. Say: "If It Is To Be – It Is Up To Me". Then take action.

My Five Senses at Work

I **Hear** the voices of so many – in the distance –
    Crying out in undying pain.
There must be a way to calm the cries –
    To dull any future refrain.

I **See** the faces of too many – right up close –
    Painted with frowns of discontent.
There must be a way to ease the tension –
    Bringing peace to those who are "over-spent".

I **Taste** the bitterness of the nectar –
    Flowing from the flowers – covered with pollution.
There must be a way to cleanse the poison –
    Safely, peacefully – without need for a revolution.

I **Feel** the sharpness of the thorns –
    That prick the innocent children at play.
There must be a way to remove the thorns –
    Keeping our children safe – by night and day.

I **Smell** the sickening aroma of inner city decay –
    Creating shallow breaths & oxygen deprivation to the brain.
There must be a way to purge the stench –
    With no dependence on the clean up – by use of acid rain.

We Must Correct It All In the Nick Of Time!!!!!

There May Come a Time

Holding a hand may be enough for a while.
There may be hugging and kissing which may be
more your style.

Then there is something that may come next.
That something is what some folk call "sex".

Others may call it "good old fashion love making".
Don't be surprised – if at times you may practice faking.

Each and every session may not allow climax to occur.
So, your own pleasure you may have to defer.

With the passing of time – some passion may diminish.
One or both may not be able to start or even finish.

"There May Come a Time" – when cuddling is all
that you do.
Just make yourself content to do whatever it takes to
get you through.

Sassy Lady

I know a "Sassy Lady".
Her name is Miss Kattie.
She sure knows how to strut her stuff.
She draws attention – sure enough.

The epitome of a graceful flamboyant style.
She wears a special infectious smile.
Her cheeks and lips are glowing apple red.
She wears a real fancy hat upon her head.

The dresses fit her curves to a sexy tee.
She wears most of them above her knee.
Miss Kattie loves to wear colors so very bright.
She could even magically illuminate the night.

Her stylish purses match the fancy shoes on her feet.
She walks real proud – as she walks down the street.
Even though Miss Kattie is now only eighty-two,
She tells everyone that she knows what to do.

Never appear or act so old – as others might expect.
Keep your youthful glow – avoid becoming a wreck.
Live each day like Sunday – by wearing your very best.
Also, take time to get your needed rest.

Eat just enough food to keep your energy flowing.
You don't need too much – 'cus you ain't still growing.
Keep your social life – inclusive of much fun along
the way.
Continue to laugh and play – age appropriately every day,

Miss Kattie says, "You are only as old as you really feel."
So, this is some good advice – just remember to
keep it real.

The Battle Scars of Life

"The Battle Scars of Life"
can eventually be overcome.
Knowing that each scar
represents encounters as we travel to and from.

Getting through each of "Life's Battles"
must truly be bravely fought.
So, all strategies must be in place,
using the tactics that we've been taught.

No more shall we live in needless regrets.
Know that each experience is ours to respectfully receive.
For "Life's Battles" are not intended to punish.
This is what we must learn to really believe.

Apply every healing ointment – to cover the scars.
Never allowing the "Battle Scars" to drive us insane.
Allow the healing to quickly take place.
So, no sign of scarring is allowed to remain.

Time to Let Go of This Stuff

One day I awakened –
surveyed the stuff in my house.
There was so much clutter –
no more room for even a mouse.

Something inside of my head said –
"Time to Let Go of This Stuff".
I had to realize that I had collected
more than enough.

Now it's time to live the life
that focuses on my special human race.
Time to let go of things
that crowd my precious living space.

Time to engage in activities
that enhance my own personal renewal.
More time must be spent in meditation –
seeking peace – and begin to refuel.

Stop Pushing Me

I feel the forces against my back.
It keeps me moving against my free-will.
A wind so strong will blow me down.
With a force this strong – I may hit the ground.

A fall too hard may break my fragile bones.
May take too long for healing to take place.
Now, I must find safe shelter from this wind.
Hope that safe haven is just around the bend.

Sometimes the forces of life are also just as strong.
The forces push so hard – from each and every angle.
Sometimes others even call me names that hurt my pride.
Keeps me always looking for a safe place to hide.

I'm not so weak, nor fearful, nor running scared.
But I do see the value of living cautious, defensive
and safe.
Knowing that the winds of life can blow me away.
It can certainly happen on any given day.

I am aware of how turbulent this life can be.
So, maintaining my own strong stance is best for me.
Never again shall I be pushed against my will.
I even know when it is time to seek shelter – sit
and be still.

Stop Pushing Me

My Oh My - My Memory Pause

A second ago it crossed my mind.
The thought was there but it went away.
Now, I can't remember what I wanted to say.

So many thoughts elude me these days.
A "Senior Moment" may be to blame.
If that's all that it is – then I'll stake my claim.

I shall not let this get the best of me.
I do all that I can to keep my mind sharp and keen.
Constant forgetfulness is not welcome on the scene.

Sure want to also keep this youthful pep in my step.
Would also love to keep my healthy glow.
Have high hopes that my "Wisdom Garden" continues
to grow.

"If you don't use it, you lose it" – just may be true.
Let no part of me become out of whack.
My mind, my body, my spirit – must all stay on track.

If occasionally I forget – let the thought soon return.
I can live with an occasional **"Memory Pause"**.
Just want to be sure that is the one and only cause.

Abandon

Abandon the negative thoughts living inside.
Abandon the things that devastate your pride.
Abandon those harmful feelings so others won't see.
Abandon those unkind words in order to be set free.

Abandon any anger that tends to appear.
Abandon any habits that are unbecoming my dear.
Abandon those fears that do hold you down.
Abandon those sad songs that make you frown.

Abandon the needless things that clutter up your life.
Abandon the childish stuff that causes you so much strife.
Abandon all the folk who try to lead you astray.
Abandon all that which does not serve to brighten
your day.

Time Is a Flying

"Time Is a Flying" – Many think it's so.

We look around and think – "Where did time go?"

Balancing work and leisure – is far from child's play.

It is wise to make the best of it – each and every day.

Things only get done by the actions that we take.

That unexpected stuff can alter the plans that we make.

Can't stash away time – to withdraw at a later date.

So, time must be wisely spent – before it's too late.

"Time Is a Flying"

Catch it if you can.

Looking for a New Song

Some days I wake up –
wondering what the day will bring.
I am seeking to do something different,
and **"Looking for a New Song"** to sing.

The current song no longer serves –
my body, mind nor soul.
I am seeking to make some changes
and needing to rip away the old.

It may take some time to prepare
and even retrain my human mind.
It may help to identify what, why, who,
when and how – as I attempt to redefine.

I am looking for a "New Song" –
that I know must be hiding in my head.
It must be a happy song for me to sing –
from the time I wake up – 'til I go to bed.

Can Not Run - Can Not Hide

"I Can Not Run – I Can Not Hide"
from this person living inside.

They follow me when I'm on the go.
Where I go – they always know.

They peek inside my every thought.
Even know what I was taught.

I have to always do things right.
'cus I am always in their sight.

I have learned – they will always be a part of me.
This has truly become my personal reality.

"I Can Not Run – I Can Not Hide"
from this person living inside.

Time to Hit the Reset Button

Time to reset the way we think.
Time to reset what we drink.

Time to reset how we live each day.
Time to reset how we tend to play.

Time to reset what we eat.
Time to reset how we accept defeat.

Time to reset how we manage our life.
Time to reset the expectations of husband or wife.

Time to reset how we spend our money.
Time to reset how we treat our "honey".

Time to reset our life's goals.
Time to reset our active roles.

Time to reset our current weight.
Time to reset how long we plan to wait.

Time to reset how we make our cash.
Time to reset how much we keep in our stash.

Time to reset when to make the most of "it".
Time to reset when to keep going or when to quit.

Old Shoes and Me - Just Kicking It

Life goes on and so do I.
No need to ask how or why.

I continue to "Just Keep Kicking It" with my old shoes.
The feet inside are as old too – as the oldest news.

No tight schedules to keep.
Wake up when I'm ready – from a restful sleep.

This day is not even prearranged – no one has
made a demand.
I can choose to walk the beach and even kick the sand.

I can even "Kick the can down the road".
The truth be told – I'm not burdened by a heavy load.

All in all – I'm happy to be free.
Finding so much peace – just to be me.

"Old Shoes and Me – Just Kicking It" – from
day to day.
So very rewarding – to be living life my way.

An Invitation to an Abundant Life

You are cordially invited
to participate in "An Abundant Life".
Be warned of pending days –
filled with mixed emotions and strife.

Giving the series of events no particular order.
Abundance of riches will eventually grow.
The natural order of things
will determine how you days will flow.

You are most capable of doing the work.
A most strong candidate for the part.
Observations have further revealed –
that you have a willing heart.

So, you will take charge and see that there is:
Order in the midst of chaos.
Love in the midst of hatred.
Freedom in the midst of oppression.
Generosity in the midst of poverty.
Light in the midst of darkness.
Fun in the midst of toil.
Knowledge in the midst of ignorance.
Happiness in the midst of sadness.
Hope in the midst of disparity.
Strength in the midst of weakness.
Life in the midst of Death.

So, this invitation does come with expectations.
You will have to employ your strength and fortitude
in order to successfully live **"An Abundant Life"**.

***

Do you accept the challenge and the invitation?

Hush – Be Still

Hush – Be Still.
Do you hear it?
Maybe you never will.

Hush – Be Still.
Do you see it?
Maybe it really can't even be seen.

Gently close your eyes.
Do you feel it?
Do you feel its gentle warmth surrounding you?
It is always there – day and night – to embrace you.

"No time to allow it in" – you say.
"Too busy doing life" – some say.
It may be time to find a secret corner:
In a closet, along a pathway, in a garden, in an attic,
in a chapel, in the arms of a loved one.

What are we looking for?

It is silence, it is golden, it is peace.
It is vanilla, it is chocolate, it is strawberry, it is pistachio.
It is any color or flavor that you might imagine it to be.

Just take a precious moment to
"Hush – Be Still".

I Must Pick

"I Must Pick" those things
that in my life must be.
It is fool hearted to waste time
on what matters not to me.

Too much precious time is spent
in search of "Fool's Gold".
Before I look around
I may have become too very old.

Then, I would tend to question
where the years have flown.
It should become no mystery
as I remember precious time that I have blown.

Now, again, I remind myself – that **"I Must Pick"** –
those things that matter most to me.
It is really "Fool Hearted" not to do so –
because I do possess "Life's Golden Key".

Time to Turn Over a New Leaf

I awakened this morning –
began reflecting on my life.
Needed some *Divine* guidance –
seeking directions in minimizing strife.

The signs did not play tricks –
by appearing in disguise.
The signs for needed changes –
have appeared before my very eyes.

It revealed that it is –
"Time to Turn Over a New Leaf".

The "old leaf" has lost its life and luster
and has actually turned brown.
It is now time for me
to moved on – to a stimulating new town.

Grandma's Secret Recipe for Happiness

Use a dash or two of **Laughter**

Throw in much – much **Patience**

Add one very big heartfelt dose of **Genuine Love**

Plop in a large scoop of **Faith**

Maintain one head full of **Understanding**

Add one large serving spoon of **Positive Thoughts**

Add a gigantic dash of **Generosity**

***

Now, mix the entire ingredients well.

Serve everyone who you meet.

***

Feel free to modify the recipe –
to make it rich and extra special.

"If I Could Touch but One Heart Today" –
If only one soul's inspiration shall ignite –
If you shall be the only one –
Then this compilation of poetry shall be well done.

If I could make but one life brighter –
If only one happiness I shall arouse –
If you shall be the only one –
Then this project's labor of love – shall be done.

When most of the wisdom I have for now has
been shared –
When all of the messages are well delivered –
When here within you've learned a special thought –
Then you have understood some of what I have taught.

When your allotted time was well spent –
When your concentration maintained its focus –
When you imagine accomplishing your life's
greatest desire –
Then, I give Thanks – for it is my goal to so inspire.

Between the Lines

May you continue to find some words of wisdom and "Food for Thought" in the following series of reflections and questions. Take time to consider ideas that may extend beyond the expressions as they appear. **"Between the Lines"** is intended for you to consider your own personal situation and think of what is expressed and even what is not expressed.

- Everything that I really know about life: We are born. We live our lives. We die. Now, before we reach the end.........
- Today is now today. Yesterday was once today. Today will also become yesterday. What do you need to do today – that you did not do yesterday?
- When your mind wanders – does it tend to follow your heart?
- Certain rituals help to sustain us. Do you have any rituals?
- The world around us – ushers in much turbulence. How much turbulence do you allow into your personal world?

- Some little things do matter. Too many little things become the ingredients for bigger things.
- Remember, an 'empty car' can't drive on fumes. Are you attempting to drive an 'empty car'?
- A crack in 'the foundation' may indicate trouble with the main structure. Watch out for the cracks.
- 'Cons' in a bottle – alcohol and drugs. 'Cons' on two legs – some men and some women too.
- The only ideas the really work for you – are the ideas that you personally put to work.
- What you exhibit outside of yourself – can really count much less than what you truly feel inside of yourself.
- Happiness can come in the form of a "sweet drink" – that you can't pour on others – without getting a few drops on yourself.
- Continue to 'feed' your faith and your troubles and doubts will soon fade away.
- Remember, a lie may make you think that you are in the clear for the present, but you may be in deep "do-do" in the future.
- Anger is only one letter short of danger.
- You must continue to focus on what really matters and dispose of the garbage that is stinking. How big of a garbage container do you need?
- Those who need "It" most – take advantage of "It" least. "It" being: education, knowledge, information, prayer ....

- "Clutterology" is practiced by more people than we can imagine. Most keep this practice behind closed doors, privacy fences, vehicles and their human mind. What are some special ways to de-clutter the human mind?
- When the minister pronounces the newly couple "Man and Wife" – it sounds as if the man (gender specific) is free to do what the heck he wants to. The Wife is to take on the role of attending to home chores. What about – the pronouncement of "Husband and Wife"? The husband's role is to also be a companion within the relationship and to take on new responsibilities as such.
- All she wanted was a wedding ring. He brought her so much more. He brought her his soiled laundry and walked back out the door.
- A party that you should never attend: A "Pity Party". You just may find yourself to be the only guest at that party.
- Some don't use make-up everyday. Not that they have perfect skin. They have just learned to love the skin that they are in.
- Love can be like "Quick Sand". It can suck you in. You can't even resist the force. You may find yourself trying to resist – until the bitter end.
- Love can quickly fade – if "Fresh Paint" is not occasionally applied.

- Love for others – really starts with loving yourself first. Self love is the solid foundation upon which to build a love for another.
- Love and like are two different feelings. You may love a person, but you do not like the things that they do. So, when saying, "I don't love you anymore" – may mean "I don't really like the things that you do".
- Relationships and marriages call for compromise and periods of inconvenience. If compromise and/or inconvenience are not acceptable for you to tolerate – you may wish to rethink your readiness for a serious relationship of any kind.
- Mistrust, disrespect, lack of intimacy and financial harmony are the top triggers of discord and relationship disconnections. Consider any others that are essential to you.
- True and unconditional love is a solid bridge to a loving connection. It may be difficult to practice unconditional anything. Expectations equate to conditions. Expectations become a part of what we desire.
- Looking for the keys to happiness? Reach into your own heart. Attempting to invade the heart of another – to locate your happiness –is too often counter-productive.
- In order to receive what you want – you must be able to articulate your wants. Your partner can only

deliver what you specifically express. Exception: If your partner is a "Mind Reader".

- Sacrifices within a relationship should be done artfully, faithfully, creatively, respectfully and endlessly.........
- There are certain "clues" that our mates leave behind, but sometimes we tend to ignore them or dismiss them. Then one day – we say, "Didn't see that coming". Duh......
- Obsessions do differ from one person to another. Some may be too annoying to over-look. Take time for the needed "conversation" – before the annoying obsession becomes an explosive situation.
- Do you like your mate from behind – as well as in front? No ifs, ands or buts about it – both views should appeal to you.
- Hint, hint – If you are having an affair and your association is visible on the street – you may want to think twice and be more discreet. You may be seen by others who are anxious to tell. Your life going forward – may feel like a living hell. On the other hand – just don't.
- Remember, from time to time it may be necessary to "Redefine your connection" within your relationship. This is one key to maintaining a long and loving relationship.
- In the silence of the human voice – "Body Language" conveys many messages. The signal

that your body sends – may be very powerful. Be aware of the messages sent – are not only by way of the words spoken, but the visual language of the human body.

- If happiness has not found you – you may want to come out of hiding.
- To nourish the body – without nourishing the mind and the soul – leaves the job incomplete.
- Holding on to grudges, hatred and old issues – is a personal decision to bring suffering upon yourself.
- Continue to say to yourself, "I am loved because I love myself first".
- If you have ever had a "Root Canal" – you certainly want it to be done right the first time. So it is with a marriage. The time taken to know all of the steps and expectations is important to getting it right the first time. There are too many "do-over's".
- Too much anger in a human – is like too much air in a balloon. Too much of either may cause one or the other to POP.
- It has been said that relationships need "A third leg". It has also been said that "Three is a crowd". Think it over. Be aware of the make or break 'power of three'.
- Know the difference between jealousy and mistrust. Jealousy is about wanting something that someone else has. Mistrust is about suspicions that something may be going on behind one's back. When someone says that, "My wife is jealous" – No, she does

not want what you have. Rather, if your behavior is suspicious – she does not trust you. Mistrust is a real deal breaker.

- It may not be wise to "Jump ship" every time the sailing get rough. If you do jump ship – you had better have a secure life boat. Then again, too many rough sailings may mean that the captain and the co-captain need some training and some intervention.
- Relationships require some "Space sharing". So, determine who you are willing to share your space with. I mean – really determine.......
- Our actions reflect the thinking that is taking place in our brain. As we observe the actions of others – we may need to be aware of the extent to which they will go to win an argument. Get to know their "anger triggers" and the extent of their "retaliation reflexes".
- No one wears the skin of another. No one can feel the pain of the pinch except the person on the receiving end. Be careful how hard you may tend to pinch another. It may not be wise to test their "retaliation reflexes".
- It has been said that, "The apple does not fall too far from the tree". In some cases – we may suspect that the tree must have moved.
- One rotten can spoil the good apples in the bowl. So, remove the rotten apple as soon as it is spotted.

- When we feel that we have 'outgrown the tiny box' – it may be wise to think of ways and work on ways – to leave 'the tiny box'.
- If we are in control – we must take responsibility. Some things we make happen, some things we let happen and some things just happen. There is no shame, no blame – only an opportunity to learn another "Life Lesson" and rise to a better place.
- Remember, one can't climb a ladder that is not upright and is lying on the ground.
- Do not allow a "creep" to creep up on you. Knowledge and awareness are your best and most reliable defenses.

Some Situations that Can Trigger Discord In Human Relations

(Listed in random order)

_Misunderstandings   _Lack of Good Communications   _Narcissism

_Lack of Proper Information   _Mistrust   _Drugs

_Fear or Fears   _Secrets   _Dependency   _Hygiene

_Isolation   _Different Beliefs   _Religion   _Denial

_Prejudices   _Expectations   _Disappointments   _Lack of Empathy

_Ruts   _Teasing   _Negative Attitudes   _Sleep Habits

_Negative Dialogue   _Anger   _Jealousy   _Envy   _Hate

_Possessiveness   _Complexes (Inferior or Superior)   _Divisiveness

_Physical and/or Mental Illness (Self or Others)   _Speculations

_Financial   _Low Achievers   _High Achievers

_Moral or Immoral Values   _Different Value Systems   _Selfishness

_Family Beliefs   _Family Values   _Jumping to Conclusions

_Racial Issues   _Disrespect   _Parenting Differences

_Pride   _Lack of Pride   _Age   _Generation Gaps

_Gender Differences   _Sexual Beliefs   _Social Issues

_Physical Differences   _Emotional Differences   _Assumptions

_Educational Differences   _Food Preferences   _Management Skills

Practice Saying the "Ten I's"

OFTEN TIMES PEOPLE say things that they wish that they could take back.

The spoken word and our actions can not be reversed. The one thing that we must learn to do – is to express forgiveness, ask for forgiveness and make amends for our mistakes. The following are some suggestions:

1. I apologize
2. I need your help
3. I misunderstood
4. I made a mistake
5. I need more information
6. I appreciate your patience
7. I did not intend to hurt you
8. I beg you for your forgiveness
9. I promise to never do that again
10. I have no idea what came over me

If these do not work – seek advice from someone who you personally know of – who is known to "Put their foot in their mouth" and manage to get out unhurt and alive. (Hint – Hint)

www.ingramcontent.com/pod-product-compliance
Lightning Source LLC
Chambersburg PA
CBHW070806100426
42742CB00012B/2265

9 781931 259040